DRAW IT:

ANIMALS

BECKY J. RADTKE

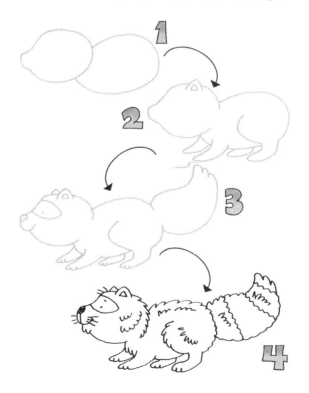

DOVER PUBLICATIONS, INC.
Mineola, New York

Bibliographical Note

Draw It! Animals is a new work, first published by Dover
Publications, Inc., in 2013.

International Standard Book Number

ISBN-13: 978-0-486-49955-0
ISBN-10: 0-486-49955-3

Manufactured in the United States by Courier Corporation
49955301   2013
www.doverpublications.com

Would you like to draw animals? In this handy book, you'll learn how to draw a chimpanzee, a koala, a rhinoceros, and a tortoise—plus many more creatures. Just follow the steps, from 1 to 4. Step 1 shows you the basic shape. Step 2 might add a face, feet, and a tail. By Step 3, you will see the entire animal. Step 4 shows you how to add details such as fur, whiskers, or spots to finish your picture. Opposite each page with the four drawing steps is another page where you can draw your animal. There's even a helpful hint for each picture!

Alligator

This critter's nostrils face upward—so it can breathe at the water's surface.

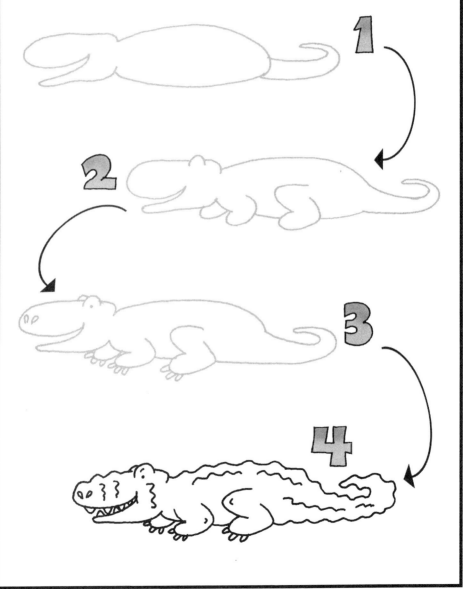

Ape

It's easy to recognize by its long arms and broad chest.

5

Bear

Don't let the burly appearance fool you—
this animal is incredibly fast.

7

Beaver

This rodent has a flat tail and does well in water because of its webbed feet.

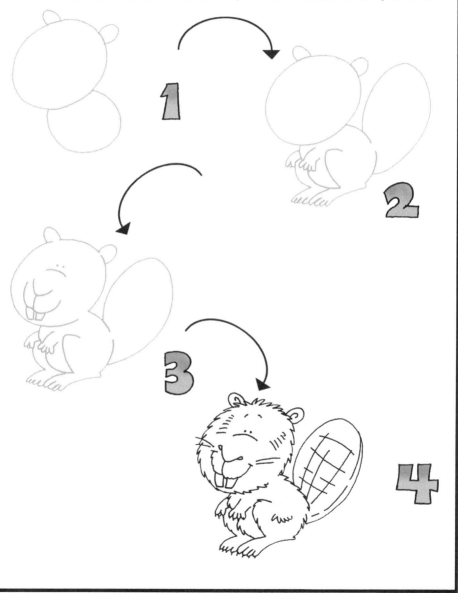

Camel

Flat, wide feet keep this desert traveler from sinking into the sand.

11

Cat

A popular pet, this animal has excellent hearing and night vision.

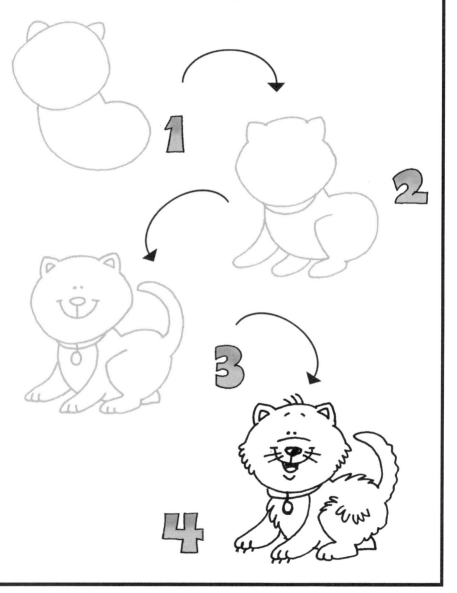

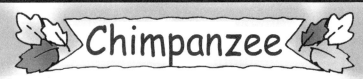

Chimpanzee

A young chimpanzee learns about safe foods to eat by watching the adults.

15

Dog

This furry friend needs training and plenty of space to exercise.

17

Duck

This male drake eats mostly vegetables, searching for food as he swims.

Eagle

This large bird has a hooked beak and powerful talons that capture prey.

21

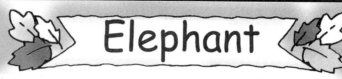

This massive mammal really does have a remarkable memory.

23

Flamingo

No one knows for sure why this wading bird stands on one leg.

Fox

This sly creature uses its tail, called a brush, as a blanket to stay warm.

27

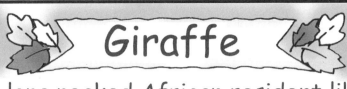

Giraffe

This long-necked African resident likes to dine on Acacia leaves.

29

Goat

Often found on a farm, this excellent jumper has four stomachs.

31

Goose

Honking sounds help this waterfowl find his way in the air and on land.

33

Hippopotamus

This barrel-bodied guy, if threatened, can become aggressive and dangerous.

Horse

This magnificent mare can take a snooze standing up or lying down.

37

Hyena

Known for its laughing sound, this social animal often lives and hunts in groups.

Kangaroo

A built-in, comfortable pouch carries her baby, called a "joey."

41

Koala

Contrary to popular opinion, this sharp-clawed climber is not a type of bear.

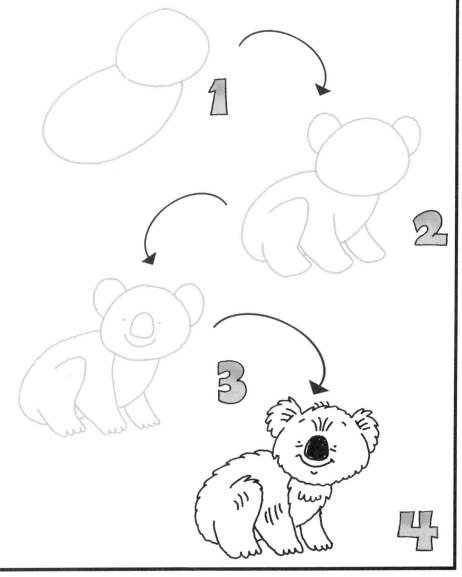

43

Leopard

This big cat prowls at night, lives alone, and is an efficient swimmer.

45

Lion

This "king of the jungle" sleeps or rests for up to twenty hours a day.

Moose

Part of the deer family, this massive fellow grows broad, distinctive antlers.

49

Ostrich

This well-known giant bird can't fly,
but it's a super-fast runner.

Owl

This creature can turn his head about three-quarters of the way around!

53

Parrot

This intelligent talker has relatives from the tropics.

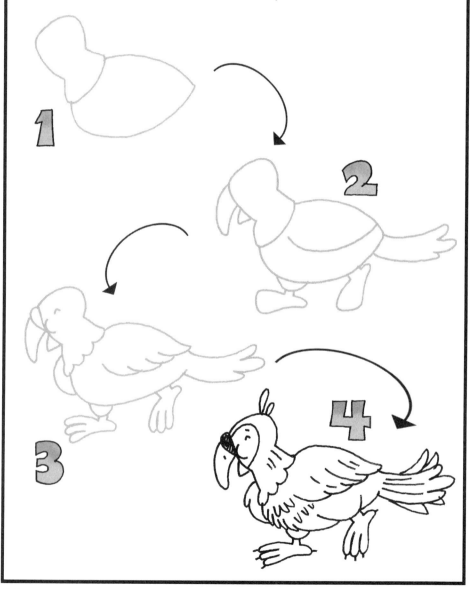

55

Penguin

Playtime includes body surfing, belly sliding, and cliff diving.

Porcupine

This waddling rodent has sharp quills
for protection against its enemies.

59

Rabbit

Called a "kit" at birth, this hairy hopper started out with no fur and closed eyes.

Raccoon

This masked animal can make a home in the forest, prairie, or city.

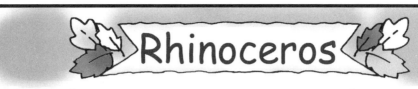

Rhinoceros

This horned beast wears mud for sun and insect protection.

Sheep

Her fine wool can be made into clothing.

67

Swan

This graceful swimmer
will find a mate for life.

Tiger

The striped pattern on this hunter is one of a kind.

Tortoise

This cold-blooded reptile carries a form of shelter on its back.

Wolf

Even though this howling creature looks like a dog, it is a flesh eater of the wild.

Zebra

Resembling a horse, this stocky mammal has night vision.